This record book belongs to _____

School _____   Phone _____

Grade _____   Room _____   Year _____

Contents

Record student names across the top.

Record dates of assessments or use a section for each quarter of the year.

Record individual proficiencies at each date. You may choose to use any system, such as check marks, a 1–4 rubric, letters, or grades.

	Cara Avery				Luis Diaz				Sam Edwards				Jayl	
	9/6	9/8	10/15	2/3	9/6	9/8	10/15	2/3	9/6	9/8	10/15	2/3	9/6	9/
4.OA.A.1	1	1	2	2	3	3	3	4	1	2	2	3	2	3
	- struggles with problems in word form - needs support with 6–9 times tables				- successful with all types of problems				- needs help decoding problems as statements				- strugg facts	

Add detailed notes throughout the year.

For a more comprehensive resource guide with tips and additional reproducibles, visit *activities.carsondellosa.com*.

ISBN 978-1-4838-1115-4
01-135147784

Math Standards At a Glance

OA

Use four operations with whole numbers to solve problems.

4.OA.A.1 Interpret a multiplication equation as a comparison. Represent verbal statements of multiplicative comparisons as multiplication equations.

4.OA.A.2 Multiply or divide to solve word problems involving multiplicative comparison, distinguishing multiplicative comparison from additive comparison.

4.OA.A.3 Solve multistep word problems posed with whole numbers and having whole-number answers using the four operations, including problems in which remainders must be interpreted. Represent these problems using equations with a letter standing for the unknown quantity. Assess the reasonableness of answers using mental computation and estimation strategies including rounding.

Gain familiarity with factors and multiples.

4.OA.B.4 Find all factor pairs for a whole number in the range 1–100. Recognize that a whole number is a multiple of each of its factors. Determine whether a given whole number in the range 1–100 is a multiple of a given one-digit number. Determine whether a given whole number in the range 1–100 is prime or composite.

Generate and analyze patterns.

4.OA.C.5 Generate a number or shape pattern that follows a given rule. Identify apparent features of the pattern that were not explicit in the rule itself.

NBT

Generalize place value understanding for multi-digit whole numbers.

4.NBT.A.1 Recognize that in a multi-digit whole number, a digit in one place represents ten times what it represents in the place to its right.

4.NBT.A.2 Read and write multi-digit whole numbers using base-ten numerals, number names, and expanded form. Compare two multi-digit numbers based on meanings of the digits in each place, using >, =, and < symbols to record the results of comparisons

4.NBT.A.3 Use place value understanding to round multi-digit whole numbers to any place.

Use place value understanding and properties of operations to perform multi-digit arithmetic.

4.NBT.B.4 Fluently add and subtract multi-digit whole numbers using the standard algorithm.

4.NBT.B.5 Multiply a whole number of up to four digits by a one-digit whole number, and multiply two two-digit numbers, using strategies based on place value and the properties of operations. Illustrate and explain the calculation by using equations, rectangular arrays, and/or area models.

4.NBT.B.6 Find whole-number quotients and remainders with up to four-digit dividends and one-digit divisors, using strategies based on place value, the properties of operations, and/or the relationship between multiplication and division. Illustrate and explain the calculation by using equations, rectangular arrays, and/or area models.

Note: Grade 4 expectations in this domain are limited to whole numbers less than or equal to 1,000,000.

NF

Extend understanding of fraction equivalence and ordering.

4.NF.A.1 Explain why a fraction a/b is equivalent to a fraction $(n \times a)/(n \times b)$ by using visual fraction models, with attention to how the number and size of the parts differ even though the two fractions themselves are the same size. Use this principle to recognize and generate equivalent fractions.

4.NF.A.2 Compare two fractions with different numerators and different denominators. Recognize that comparisons are valid only when the two fractions refer to the same whole. Record the results of comparisons with symbols >, =, or <, and justify the conclusions.

Build fractions from unit fractions by applying and extending previous understandings of operations on whole numbers.

4.NF.B.3 Understand a fraction a/b with $a > 1$ as a sum of fractions $1/b$.

4.NF.B.3a Understand addition and subtraction of fractions as joining and separating parts referring to the same whole.

4.NF.B.3b Decompose a fraction into a sum of fractions with the same denominator in more than one way, recording each decomposition by an equation. Justify decompositions.

4.NF.B.3c Add and subtract mixed numbers with like denominators.

4.NF.B.3d Solve word problems involving addition and subtraction of fractions referring to the same whole and having like denominators.

4.NF.B.4 Apply and extend previous understandings of multiplication to multiply a fraction by a whole number.

4.NF.B.4a Understand a fraction a/b as a multiple of $1/b$.

4.NF.B.4b Understand a multiple of a/b as a multiple of $1/b$, and use this understanding to multiply a fraction by a whole number. (In general, $n \times (a/b) = (n \times a)/b$.)

4.NF.B.4c Solve word problems involving multiplication of a fraction by a whole number.

Understand decimal notation for fractions, and compare decimal fractions.

4.NF.C.5 Express a fraction with denominator 10 as an equivalent fraction with denominator 100, and use this technique to add two fractions with respective denominators 10 and 100.

4.NF.C.6 Use decimal notation for fractions with denominators 10 or 100.

4.NF.C.7 Compare two decimals to hundredths by reasoning about their size. Recognize that comparisons are valid only when the two decimals refer to the same whole. Record the results of comparisons with the symbols >, =, or <, and justify the conclusions.

Note: Grade 4 expectations in this domain are limited to fractions with denominators 2, 3, 4, 5, 6, 8, 10, 12, and 100.

Solve problems involving measurement and conversion of measurements from a larger unit to a smaller unit.

4.MD.A.1 Know relative sizes of measurement units within one system of units including km, m, cm; kg, g; lb, oz.; l, ml; hr, min, sec. Within a single system of measurement, express measurements in a larger unit in terms of a smaller unit. Record measurement equivalents in a two-column table.

4.MD.A.2 Use the four operations to solve word problems involving distances, intervals of time, liquid volumes, masses of objects, and money, including problems involving simple fractions or decimals, and problems that require expressing measurements given in a larger unit in terms of a smaller unit. Represent measurement quantities using diagrams such as number line diagrams that feature a measurement scale.

4.MD.A.3 Apply the area and perimeter formulas for rectangles in real world and mathematical problems.

Represent and interpret data.

4.MD.B.4 Make a line plot to display a data set of measurements in fractions of a unit (1/2, 1/4, 1/8). Solve problems involving addition and subtraction of fractions by using information presented in line plots.

Geometric measurement: understand concepts of angle and measure angles.

4.MD.C.5 Recognize angles as geometric shapes that are formed wherever two rays share a common endpoint, and understand concepts of angle measurement:

    4.MD.C.5a An angle is measured with reference to a circle with its center at the common endpoint of the rays, by considering the fraction of the circular arc between the points where the two rays intersect the circle. An angle that turns through 1/360 of a circle is called a "one-degree angle" and can be used to measure angles.

    4.MD.C.5b An angle that turns through n one-degree angles is said to have an angle measure of n degrees.

4.MD.C.6 Measure angles in whole-number degrees using a protractor. Sketch angles of specified measure.

4.MD.C.7 Recognize angle measure as additive. When an angle is decomposed into non-overlapping parts, the angle measure of the whole is the sum of the angle measures of the parts. Solve addition and subtraction problems to find unknown angles on a diagram in real world and mathematical problems.

Draw and identify lines and angles, and classify shapes and properties of their lines and angles.

4.G.A.1 Draw points, lines, line segments, rays, angles (right, acute, obtuse), and perpendicular and parallel lines. Identify these in two-dimensional figures.

4.G.A.2 Classify two-dimensional figures based on the presence or absence of parallel or perpendicular lines, or the presence or absence of angles of a specified size. Recognize right triangles as a category, and identify right triangles.

4.G.A.3 Recognize a line of symmetry for a two-dimensional figure as a line across the figure such that the figure can be folded along the line into matching parts. Identify line-symmetric figures and draw lines of symmetry.

Language Arts Standards At a Glance

Key Ideas and Details

RL.4.1 Refer to details and examples in a text when explaining what the text says explicitly and when drawing inferences from the text.

RL.4.2 Determine a theme of a story, drama, or poem from details in the text; summarize the text.

RL.4.3 Describe in depth a character, setting, or event in a story or drama, drawing on specific details in the text.

Craft and Structure

RL.4.4 Determine the meaning of words and phrases as they are used in a text, including those that allude to significant characters found in mythology.

RL.4.5 Explain major differences between poems, drama, and prose, and refer to the structural elements of poems and drama when writing or speaking about a text.

RL.4.6 Compare and contrast the point of view from which different stories are narrated, including the difference between first- and third-person narrations.

Integration of Knowledge and Ideas

RL.4.7 Make connections between the text of a story or drama and a visual or oral presentation of the text, identifying where each version reflects specific descriptions and directions in the text.

RL.4.8 (not applicable to literature)

RL.4.9 Compare and contrast the treatment of similar themes and topics and patterns of events in stories, myths, and traditional literature from different cultures.

Range of Reading and Level of Text Complexity

RL.4.10 By the end of the year, read and comprehend literature, including stories, dramas, and poetry, in the grades 4–5 text complexity band proficiently, with scaffolding as needed at the high end of the range.

Language Arts Standards At a Glance

Key Ideas and Details

RI.4.1 Refer to details and examples in a text when explaining what the text says explicitly and when drawing inferences from the text.

RI.4.2 Determine the main idea of a text and explain how it is supported by key details; summarize the text.

RI.4.3 Explain events, procedures, ideas, or concepts in a historical, scientific, or technical text, including what happened and why, based on specific information in the text.

Craft and Structure

RI.4.4 Determine the meaning of general academic and domain-specific words or phrases in a text relevant to a *grade 4 topic or subject area*.

RI.4.5 Describe the overall structure of events, ideas, concepts, or information in a text or part of a text.

RI.4.6 Compare and contrast a firsthand and secondhand account of the same event or topic; describe the differences in focus and the information provided.

Integration of Knowledge and Ideas

RI.4.7 Interpret information presented visually, orally, or quantitatively and explain how the information contributes to an understanding of the text in which it appears.

RI.4.8 Explain how an author uses reasons and evidence to support particular points in a text.

RI.4.9 Integrate information from two texts on the same topic in order to write or speak about the subject knowledgeably.

Range of Reading and Level of Text Complexity

RI.4.10 By the end of year, read and comprehend informational texts, including history/social studies, science, and technical texts, in the grades 4–5 text complexity band proficiently, with scaffolding as needed at the high end of the range.

Phonics and Word Recognition

RF.4.3 Know and apply grade-level phonics and word analysis skills in decoding words.

    RF.4.3a Use combined knowledge of all letter-sound correspondences, syllabication patterns, and morphology to read accurately unfamiliar multisyllabic words in context and out of context.

Fluency

RF.4.4 Read with sufficient accuracy and fluency to support comprehension.

    RF.4.4a Read grade-level text with purpose and understanding.

    RF.4.4b Read grade-level prose and poetry orally with accuracy, appropriate rate, and expression on successive readings.

    RF.4.4c Use context to confirm or self-correct word recognition and understanding, rereading as necessary.

Text Types and Purposes

W.4.1 Write opinion pieces on topics or texts, supporting a point of view with reasons and information.

    W.4.1a Introduce a topic or text clearly, state an opinion, and create an organizational structure in which related ideas are grouped to support the writer's purpose.

    W.4.1b Provide reasons that are supported by facts and details.

    W.4.1c Link opinion and reasons using words and phrases.

    W.4.1d Provide a concluding statement or section related to the opinion presented.

W.4.2 Write informative/explanatory texts to examine a topic and convey ideas and information clearly.

    W.4.2a Introduce a topic clearly and group related information in paragraphs and sections; include formatting, illustrations, and multimedia when useful to aiding comprehension.

    W.4.2b Develop the topic with facts, definitions, concrete details, quotations, or other information and examples related to the topic.

    W.4.2c Link ideas within categories of information using words and phrases.

    W.4.2d Use precise language and domain-specific vocabulary to inform about or explain the topic.

    W.4.2e Provide a concluding statement or section related to the information or explanation presented.

W.4.3 Write narratives to develop real or imagined experiences or events using effective technique, descriptive details, and clear event sequences.

    W.4.3a Orient the reader by establishing a situation and introducing a narrator and/or characters; organize an event sequence that unfolds naturally.

    W.4.3b Use dialogue and description to develop experiences and events or show the responses of characters to situations.

    W.4.3c Use a variety of transitional words and phrases to manage the sequence of events.

    W.4.3d Use concrete words and phrases and sensory details to convey experiences and events precisely.

    W.4.3e Provide a conclusion that follows from the narrated experiences or events.

Production and Distribution of Writing

W.4.4 Produce clear and coherent writing in which the development and organization are appropriate to task, purpose, and audience.

W.4.5 With guidance and support from peers and adults, develop and strengthen writing as needed by planning, revising, and editing.

W.4.6 With some guidance and support from adults, use technology, including the Internet, to produce and publish writing as well as to interact and collaborate with others; demonstrate sufficient command of keyboarding skills to type a minimum of one page in a single sitting.

Research to Build and Present Knowledge

W.4.7 Conduct short research projects that build knowledge through investigation of different aspects of a topic.

W.4.8 Recall relevant information from experiences or gather relevant information from print and digital sources; take notes and categorize information, and provide a list of sources.

W.4.9 Draw evidence from literary or informational texts to support analysis, reflection, and research.

W.4.9a Apply grade 4 Reading standards to literature.

W.4.9b Apply grade 4 Reading standards to informational texts.

Range of Writing
W.4.10 Write routinely over extended time frames (time for research, reflection, and revision) and shorter time frames (a single sitting or a day or two) for a range of discipline-specific tasks, purposes, and audiences.

Comprehension and Collaboration
SL.4.1 Engage effectively in a range of collaborative discussions (one-on-one, in groups, and teacher-led) with diverse partners on *grade 4 topics and texts*, building on others' ideas and expressing their own clearly.

SL.4.1a Come to discussions prepared, having read or studied required material; explicitly draw on that preparation and other information known about the topic to explore ideas under discussion.

SL.4.1b Follow agreed-upon rules for discussions and carry out assigned roles.

SL.4.1c Pose and respond to specific questions to clarify or follow up on information, and make comments that contribute to the discussion and link to the remarks of others.

SL.4.1d Review the key ideas expressed and explain their own ideas and understanding in light of the discussion.

SL.4.2 Paraphrase portions of a text read aloud or information presented in diverse media and formats, including visually, quantitatively, and orally.

SL.4.3 Identify the reasons and evidence a speaker provides to support particular points.

Presentation of Knowledge and Ideas
SL.4.4 Report on a topic or text, tell a story, or recount an experience in an organized manner, using appropriate facts and relevant, descriptive details to support main ideas or themes; speak clearly at an understandable pace.

SL.4.5 Add audio recordings and visual displays to presentations when appropriate to enhance the development of main ideas or themes.

SL.4.6 Differentiate between contexts that call for formal English and situations where informal discourse is appropriate; use formal English when appropriate to task and situation.

Conventions of Standard English
L.4.1 Demonstrate command of the conventions of standard English grammar and usage when writing or speaking.

L.4.1a Use relative pronouns and relative adverbs.

L.4.1b Form and use the progressive verb tenses.

L.4.1c Use modal auxiliaries to convey various conditions.

L.4.1d Order adjectives within sentences according to conventional patterns.

L.4.1e Form and use prepositional phrases.

L.4.1f Produce complete sentences, recognizing and correcting inappropriate fragments and run-ons.

L.4.1g Correctly use frequently confused words.

L.4.2 Demonstrate command of the conventions of standard English capitalization, punctuation, and spelling when writing.

L.4.2a Use correct capitalization.

L.4.2b Use commas and quotation marks to mark direct speech and quotations from a text.

L.4.2c Use a comma before a coordinating conjunction in a compound sentence.

L.4.2d Spell grade-appropriate words correctly, consulting references as needed.

Knowledge of Language
L.4.3 Use knowledge of language and its conventions when writing, speaking, reading, or listening.

L.4.3a Choose words and phrases to convey ideas precisely.

L.4.3b Choose punctuation for effect.

L.4.3c Differentiate between contexts that call for formal English and situations where informal discourse is appropriate.

Vocabulary Acquisition and Use
L.4.4 Determine or clarify the meaning of unknown and multiple-meaning word and phrases based on *grade 4 reading and content*, choosing flexibly from a range of strategies.

L.4.4a Use context as a clue to the meaning of a word or phrase.

L.4.4b Use common, grade-appropriate Greek and Latin affixes and roots as clues to the meaning of a word.

L.4.4c Consult reference materials, both print and digital, to find the pronunciation and determine or clarify the precise meaning of key words and phrases.

L.4.5 Demonstrate understanding of figurative language, word relationships, and nuances in word meanings.

L.4.5a Explain the meaning of simple similes and metaphors in context.

L.4.5b Recognize and explain the meaning of common idioms, adages, and proverbs.

L.4.5c Demonstrate understanding of words by relating them to their opposites (antonyms) and to words with similar but not identical meanings (synonyms).

L.4.6 Acquire and use accurately grade-appropriate general academic and domain-specific words and phrases, including those that signal precise actions, emotions, or states of being and that are basic to a particular topic.

Operations and Algebraic Thinking

4.OA.A.1 Interpret a multiplication equation as a comparison, e.g., interpret $35 = 5 \times 7$ as a statement that 35 is 5 times as many as 7 and 7 times as many as 5. Represent verbal statements of multiplicative comparisons as multiplication equations.

4.OA.A.2 Multiply or divide to solve word problems involving multiplicative comparison, e.g., by using drawings and equations with a symbol for the unknown number to represent the problem, distinguishing multiplicative comparison from additive comparison.

4.OA.A.3 Solve multistep word problems posed with whole numbers and having whole-number answers using the four operations, including problems in which remainders must be interpreted. Represent these problems using equations with a letter standing for the unknown quantity. Assess the reasonableness of answers using mental computation and estimation strategies including rounding.

4.OA.B.4 Find all factor pairs for a whole number in the range 1–100. Recognize that a whole number is a multiple of each of its factors. Determine whether a given whole number in the range 1–100 is a multiple of a given one-digit number. Determine whether a given whole number in the range 1–100 is prime or composite.

4.OA.C.5 Generate a number or shape pattern that follows a given rule. Identify apparent features of the pattern that were not explicit in the rule itself. *For example, given the rule "Add 3" and the starting number 1, generate terms in the resulting sequence and observe that the terms appear to alternate between odd and even numbers. Explain informally why the numbers will continue to alternate in this way.*

Standards Crosswalk

Third Grade

Operations and Algebraic Thinking

Represent and solve problems involving multiplication and division.
- Interpret products of whole numbers.
- Interpret whole-number quotients of whole numbers.
- Use multiplication and division within 100 to solve word problems.
  Determine the unknown whole number in a multiplication or division equation relating three whole numbers.

Understand properties of multiplication and the relationship between multiplication and division.
- Apply properties of operations as strategies to multiply and divide.
- Understand division as an unknown-factor problem.

Multiply and divide within 100.
- Fluently multiply and divide within 100.
- Memorize all products of two one-digit numbers.

Solve problems involving the four operations, and identify and explain patterns in arithmetic.
- Use the four operations to solve two-step word problems with a variable used to represent the unknown quantity.
- Use strategies to decide if an answer is reasonable.
- Identify arithmetic patterns and explain them using properties of operations.

Fifth Grade

Operations and Algebraic Thinking

Write and interpret numerical expressions.
- Form and solve expressions with parentheses, brackets, or braces.
- Write and interpret simple numerical expressions.

Analyze patterns and relationships.
- Use given rules to generate two numerical patterns.
- Form ordered pairs from numerical patterns, and graph the ordered pairs on a coordinate plane.

4.OA.A.1					
4.OA.A.2					
4.OA.A.3					
4.OA.B.4					
4.OA.C.5					

4.OA.A.1				
4.OA.A.2				
4.OA.A.3				
4.OA.B.4				
4.OA.C.5				

4.OA.A.1					
4.OA.A.2					
4.OA.A.3					
4.OA.B.4					
4.OA.C.5					

Number and Operations in Base Ten

4.NBT.A.1 Recognize that in a multi-digit whole number, a digit in one place represents ten times what it represents in the place to its right. *For example, recognize that 700 ÷ 70 = 10 by applying concepts of place value and division.*

4.NBT.A.2 Read and write multi-digit whole numbers using base-ten numerals, number names, and expanded form. Compare two multi-digit numbers based on meanings of the digits in each place, using >, =, and < symbols to record the results of comparisons.

4.NBT.A.3 Use place value understanding to round multi-digit whole numbers to any place.

4.NBT.B.4 Fluently add and subtract multi-digit whole numbers using the standard algorithm.

4.NBT.B.5 Multiply a whole number of up to four digits by a one-digit whole number, and multiply two two-digit nubers, using strategies based on place value and the properties of operations. Illustrate and explain the calculation by using equations, rectangular arrays, and/or area models.

4.NBT.B.6 Find whole-number quotients and remainders with up to four-digit dividends and one-digit divisors, using strategies based on place value, the properties of operations, and/or the relationship between multiplication and division. Illustrate and explain the calculation by using equations, rectangular arrays, and/or area models.

Note: Grade 4 expectations in this domain are limited to whole numbers less than or equal to 1,000,000.

Standards Crosswalk

Third Grade
Number and Operations in Base Ten
Use place value understanding and properties of operations to perform multi-digit arithmetic.
- Round whole numbers to the nearest 10 or 100.
- Fluently add and subtract within 1000.
- Multiply one-digit whole numbers by multiples of 10 from 10–90.

Fifth Grade
Number and Operations in Base Ten
Understand the place value system.
- Understand that each place value is ten times larger than the place to the right, and one-tenth as large as the place to the left.
- Explain patterns in the number of zeros in a product when multiplying by a power of 10, and in the placement of the decimal point when a decimal is multiplied or divided by a power of 10.
- Use whole-number exponents to denote powers of 10.
- Read and write decimals to thousandths using base-ten numerals, words, and expanded form.
- Compare two decimals to the thousandths place using >, =, and <.
- Round decimals to any place.

Perform operations with multi-digit whole numbers and with decimals to hundredths.
- Fluently multiply multi-digit whole numbers.
- Find whole-number quotients by dividing up to four-digit dividends by two-digit divisors.
- Add, subtract, multiply, and divide decimals to the hundredths place.

4.NBT.A.1																						
4.NBT.A.2																						
4.NBT.A.3																						
4.NBT.B.4																						
4.NBT.B.5																						
4.NBT.B.6																						

4.NBT.A.1						
4.NBT.A.2						
4.NBT.A.3						
4.NBT.B.4						
4.NBT.B.5						
4.NBT.B.6						

4.NBT.A.1					
4.NBT.A.2					
4.NBT.A.3					
4.NBT.B.4					
4.NBT.B.5					
4.NBT.B.6					

Number and Operations—Fractions

4.NF.A.1 Explain why a fraction a/b is equivalent to a fraction $(n \times a)/(n \times b)$ by using visual fraction models, with attention to how the number and size of the parts differ even though the two fractions themselves are the same size. Use this principle to recognize and generate equivalent fractions.

4.NF.A.2 Compare two fractions with different numerators and different denominators, e.g., by creating common denominators or numerators, or by comparing to a benchmark fraction such as 1/2. Recognize that comparisons are valid only when the two fractions refer to the same whole. Record the results of comparisons with symbols >, =, or <, and justify the conclusions, e.g., by using a visual fraction model.

4.NF.B.3 Understand a fraction a/b with $a > 1$ as a sum of fractions $1/b$.

4.NF.B.3a Understand addition and subtraction of fractions as joining and separating parts referring to the same whole.

4.NF.B.3b Decompose a fraction into a sum of fractions with the same denominator in more than one way, recording each decomposition by an equation. Justify decompositions, e.g., by using a visual fraction model. *Examples: 3/8 = 1/8 + 1/8 + 1/8; 3/8 = 1/8 + 2/8; 2 1/8 = 1 + 1 + 1/8 = 8/8 + 8/8 + 1/8.*

4.NF.B.3c Add and subtract mixed numbers with like denominators, e.g., by replacing each mixed number with an equivalent fraction, and/or by using properties of operations and the relationship between addition and subtraction.

4.NF.B.3d Solve word problems involving addition and subtraction of fractions referring to the same whole and having like denominators, e.g., by using visual fraction models and equations to represent the problem.

4.NF.B.4 Apply and extend previous understandings of multiplication to multiply a fraction by a whole number.

4.NF.B.4a Understand a fraction a/b as a multiple of $1/b$. For example, use a visual fraction model to represent 5/4 as the product 5 × (1/4), recording the conclusion by the equation 5/4 = 5 × (1/4).

4.NF.B.4b Understand a multiple of a/b as a multiple of $1/b$, and use this understanding to multiply a fraction by a whole number. For example, use a visual fraction model to express 3 × (2/5) as 6 × (1/5), recognizing this product as 6/5. (In general, $n \times (a/b) = (n \times a)/b$.)

4.NF.B.4c Solve word problems involving multiplication of a fraction by a whole number, e.g., by using visual fraction models and equations to represent the problem. For example, if each person at a party will eat 3/8 of a pound of roast beef, and there will be 5 people at the party, how many pounds of roast beef will be needed? Between what two whole numbers does your answer lie?

4.NF.C.5 Express a fraction with denominator 10 as an equivalent fraction with denominator 100, and use this technique to add two fractions with respective denominators 10 and 100. *For example, express 3/10 as 30/100, and add 3/10 + 4/100 = 34/100.*

4.NF.C.6 Use decimal notation for fractions with denominators 10 or 100. *For example, rewrite 0.62 as 62/100; describe a length as 0.62 meters; locate 0.62 on a number line diagram.*

4.NF.C.7 Compare two decimals to hundredths by reasoning about their size. Recognize that comparisons are valid only when the two decimals refer to the same whole. Record the results of comparisons with the symbols >, =, or <, and justify the conclusions, e.g., by using a visual model.

Note: Grade 4 expectations in this domain are limited to fractions with denominators 2, 3, 4, 5, 6, 8, 10, 12, and 100.

Standards Crosswalk

Third Grade
Number and Operations—Fractions
Develop understanding of fractions as numbers.
- Recognize fractions as equal parts of a whole.
- Understand the significance of numerators and denominators.
- Represent a fraction on a number line from 0 to 1.
- Draw and divide a number line into equal parts in order to represent a fraction.
- Recognize and form simple equivalent fractions.
- Express whole numbers as fractions.
- Compare fractions that have the same numerator or same denominator using >, =, and <.

Fifth Grade
Number and Operations—Fractions
Use equivalent fractions as a strategy to add and subtract fractions.
- Add and subtract fractions and mixed numbers with unlike denominators using equivalent fractions.
- Solve word problems by adding and subtracting fractions.

Apply and extend previous understandings of multiplication and division to multiply and divide fractions.
- Understand that a fraction is the division of the numerator by the denominator.
- Solve division word problems where the answer is a fraction or a mixed number.
- Multiply a fraction or a whole number by a fraction.
- Find the area of a rectangle with fractional side lengths.
- Understand how multiplying by fractions affects the size of the product.
- Divide unit fractions by whole numbers and whole numbers by unit fractions.

4.NF.A.1																			
4.NF.A.2																			
4.NF.B.3																			
4.NF.B.4																			
4.NF.C.5																			
4.NF.C.6																			
4.NF.C.7																			

4.NF.A.1																			
4.NF.A.2																			
4.NF.B.3																			
4.NF.B.4																			
4.NF.C.5																			
4.NF.C.6																			
4.NF.C.7																			

4.NF.A.1																			
4.NF.A.2																			
4.NF.B.3																			
4.NF.B.4																			
4.NF.C.5																			
4.NF.C.6																			
4.NF.C.7																			

Measurement and Data

4.MD.A.1 Know relative sizes of measurement units within one system of units including km, m, cm; kg, g; lb, oz.; l, ml; hr, min, sec. Within a single system of measurement, express measurements in a larger unit in terms of a smaller unit. Record measurement equivalents in a two-column table. *For example, know that 1 ft is 12 times as long as 1 in. Express the length of a 4 ft snake as 48 in. Generate a conversion table for feet and inches listing the number pairs (1, 12), (2, 24), (3, 36), ...*

4.MD.A.2 Use the four operations to solve word problems involving distances, intervals of time, liquid volumes, masses of objects, and money, including problems involving simple fractions or decimals, and problems that require expressing measurements given in a larger unit in terms of a smaller unit. Represent measurement quantities using diagrams such as number line diagrams that feature a measurement scale.

4.MD.A.3 Apply the area and perimeter formulas for rectangles in real world and mathematical problems. *For example, find the width of a rectangular room given the area of the flooring and the length, by viewing the area formula as a multiplication equation with an unknown factor.*

4.MD.B.4 Make a line plot to display a data set of measurements in fractions of a unit (1/2, 1/4, 1/8). Solve problems involving addition and subtraction of fractions by using information presented in line plots. *For example, from a line plot find and interpret the difference in length between the longest and shortest specimens in an insect collection.*

4.MD.C.5 Recognize angles as geometric shapes that are formed wherever two rays share a common endpoint, and understand concepts of angle measurement:
    4.MD.C.5a An angle is measured with reference to a circle with its center at the common endpoint of the rays, by considering the fraction of the circular arc between the points where the two rays intersect the circle. An angle that turns through 1/360 of a circle is called a "one-degree angle" and can be used to measure angles.
    4.MD.C.5b An angle that turns through *n* one-degree angles is said to have an angle measure of *n* degrees.

4.MD.C.6 Measure angles in whole-number degrees using a protractor. Sketch angles of specified measure.

4.MD.C.7 Recognize angle measure as additive. When an angle is decomposed into non-overlapping parts, the angle measure of the whole is the sum of the angle measures of the parts. Solve addition and subtraction problems to find unknown angles on a diagram in real world and mathematical problems, e.g., by using an equation with a symbol for the unknown angle measure.

_____

_____

_____

_____

Standards Crosswalk

Third Grade

Measurement and Data

Solve problems involving measurement and estimation of intervals of time, liquid volumes, and masses of objects.

- Tell and write time to the nearest minute.
- Measure time intervals in minutes.
- Solve word problems involving addition and subtraction of time intervals in minutes.
- Measure and estimate liquid volume and mass using grams, kilograms, and liters.
- Solve volume and mass word problems given in the same units.

Represent and interpret data.

- Draw scaled picture and bar graphs to represent several categories.
- Analyze graphs to solve one- and two-step problems.
- Measure lengths to halves and fourths of an inch.
- Show fractional measurement data by creating line plots.

Geometric measurement: understand concepts of area and relate area to multiplication and to addition.

- Recognize area as an attribute of plane figures.
- Understand the concept of a square unit.
- Find area by counting unit squares and laying square units side by side without gaps or overlaps.
- Relate area to the operations of multiplication and addition in real world problems, using tiling and area models.
- Find areas of rectilinear figures by dividing them into non-overlapping rectangles and adding the areas of the rectangles.

Geometric measurement: recognize perimeter as an attribute of plane figures and distinguish between linear and area measures.

- Find perimeters of polygons.
- Use perimeter to unknown side lengths.
- Exhibit rectangles with the same perimeter and different areas or vice versa.

Fifth Grade

Measurement and Data

Convert like measurement units within a given measurement system.

- Convert measurement units within a measurement system.

Represent and interpret data.

- Make a line plot displaying fractions.
- Solve problems involving fifth-grade fraction operations on line plot data.

Geometric measurement: understand concepts of volume and relate volume to multiplication and to addition.

- Understand the concept of volume.
- Recognize one cubic unit of volume.
- Understand that volume is measured using cubic units to fill a solid figure with no gaps or overlaps.
- Measure volume using various units.
- Understand and apply the formulas $V = l \times w \times h$ and $V = b \times h$ to find the volume of rectangular prisms.
- Find the volume of complex solid figures by finding the volumes of rectangular prisms within the figure and adding them together.

4.MD.A.1																				

4.MD.A.2																				

4.MD.A.3																				

4.MD.B.4																				

4.MD.C.5																				

4.MD.C.6																				

4.MD.C.7																				

4.MD.A.1					
4.MD.A.2					
4.MD.A.3					
4.MD.B.4					
4.MD.C.5					
4.MD.C.6					
4.MD.C.7					

34

4.MD.A.1															
4.MD.A.2															
4.MD.A.3															
4.MD.B.4															
4.MD.C.5															
4.MD.C.6															
4.MD.C.7															

Geometry

4.G.A.1 Draw points, lines, line segments, rays, angles (right, acute, obtuse), and perpendicular and parallel lines. Identify these in two-dimensional figures.

4.G.A.2 Classify two-dimensional figures based on the presence or absence of parallel or perpendicular lines, or the presence or absence of angles of a specified size. Recognize right triangles as a category, and identify right triangles.

4.G.A.3 Recognize a line of symmetry for a two-dimensional figure as a line across the figure such that the figure can be folded along the line into matching parts. Identify line-symmetric figures and draw lines of symmetry.

Standards Crosswalk

Third Grade

Geometry

Reason with shapes and their attributes.
- Understand that shapes in different categories may share attributes, and that the shared attributes can define a larger category.
- Recognize rhombuses, rectangles, and squares as examples of quadrilaterals, and draw examples of quadrilaterals that do not belong to any of these subcategories.
- Partition shapes into parts with equal areas.
- Express the area of each part of a partition as a unit fraction of the whole.

Fifth Grade

Geometry

Graph points on the coordinate plane to solve real-world and mathematical problems.
- Understand a coordinate system and coordinates.
- Plot ordered pairs in the first quadrant of the coordinate plane.
- Use points to represent real-world problems and interpret the value of points in the context of the data they represent.

Classify two-dimensional figures into categories based on their properties.
- Recognize that all two-dimensional figures within a subcategory share the same attributes of the larger category.
- Classify two-dimensional figures in a hierarchy based on properties.

4.G.A.1

4.G.A.2

4.G.A.3

4.G.A.1

4.G.A.2

4.G.A.3

4.G.A.1

4.G.A.2

4.G.A.3

Reading Standards for Literature

RL.4.1 — Refer to details and examples in a text when explaining what the text says explicitly and when drawing inferences from the text.

RL.4.2 — Determine a theme of a story, drama, or poem from details in the text; summarize the text.

RL.4.3 — Describe in depth a character, setting, or event in a story or drama, drawing on specific details in the text (e.g., a character's thoughts, words, or actions).

RL.4.4 — Determine the meaning of words and phrases as they are used in a text, including those that allude to significant characters found in mythology (e.g., Herculean).

RL.4.5 — Explain major differences between poems, drama, and prose, and refer to the structural elements of poems (e.g., verse, rhythm, meter) and drama (e.g., casts of characters, settings, descriptions, dialogue, stage directions) when writing or speaking about a text.

RL.4.6 — Compare and contrast the point of view from which different stories are narrated, including the difference between first- and third-person narrations.

RL.4.7 — Make connections between the text of a story or drama and a visual or oral presentation of the text, identifying where each version reflects specific descriptions and directions in the text.

RL.4.8 — (Not applicable to literature)

RL.4.9 — Compare and contrast the treatment of similar themes and topics (e.g., opposition of good and evil) and patterns of events (e.g., the quest) in stories, myths, and traditional literature from different cultures.

RL.4.10 — By the end of the year, read stand comprehend literature, including stories, dramas, and poetry, in the grades 4–5 text complexity band proficiently, with scaffolding as needed at the high end of the range.

Standards Crosswalk

Third Grade
Reading: Literature
Key Ideas and Details
- Refer to text to ask and answer questions to demonstrate understanding.
- Recount stories, including fables, folktales, and myths from diverse cultures.
- Use key details to determine the central message, lesson, or moral in a text.
- Describe characters in a story and explain how their actions contribute to the sequence of events.

Craft and Structure
- Distinguish literal from nonliteral language when determining the meaning of words and phrases in a text.
- Refer to parts of stories, dramas, and poems when writing or speaking about a text, using terms such as *chapter*, *scene*, and *stanza.*
- Describe how each successive part of a story, drama, or poem builds on earlier sections.
- Distinguish their own points of view from those of the narrator or characters.

Integration of Knowledge and Ideas
- Explain how its illustrations support what is conveyed in the text.
- Compare and contrast the themes, settings, and plots of stories written by the same author about the same or similar characters.

Range of Reading and Level of Text Complexity
- By the end of the year, read and comprehend literature independently at the high end of the grades 2–3 text complexity band.

Fifth Grade
Reading: Literature
Key Ideas and Details
- Use quotes and evidence from a text to explain and draw inferences.
- Use specific details to determine the theme of a text, including character responses and reflections.
- Summarize a text.
- Compare and contrast two or more characters, settings, or events in a story or drama, drawing on specific details in the text.

Craft and Structure
- Determine the meaning of words and phrases in a text, including figurative language.
- Explain the connection between chapters, scenes, and stanzas as part of a text's structure.
- Describe how point of view affects descriptions of events.

Integration of Knowledge and Ideas
- Analyze how visual and multimedia elements contribute to the meaning, tone, or beauty of a text.
- Compare and contrast the approach to similar themes and topics in stories from the same genre.

Range of Reading and Level of Text Complexity
- By the end of the year, independently read and comprehend literature at the high end of the grades 4–5 text complexity band.

_____

_____

_____

_____

_____

_____

_____

_____

RL.4.1																			
RL.4.2																			
RL.4.3																			
RL.4.4																			
RL.4.5																			
RL.4.6																			
RL.4.7																			
RL.4.9																			
RL.4.10																			

RL.4.1				
RL.4.2				
RL.4.3				
RL.4.4				
RL.4.5				
RL.4.6				
RL.4.7				
RL.4.9				
RL.4.10				

RL.4.1																			
RL.4.2																			
RL.4.3																			
RL.4.4																			
RL.4.5																			
RL.4.6																			
RL.4.7																			
RL.4.9																			
RL.4.10																			

Reading Standards for Informational Text

RI.4.1 Refer to details and examples in a text when explaining what the text says explicitly and when drawing inferences from the text.

RI.4.2 Determine the main idea of a text and explain how it is supported by key details; summarize the text.

RI.4.3 Explain events, procedures, ideas, or concepts in a historical, scientific, or technical text, including what happened and why, based on specific information in the text.

RI.4.4 Determine the meaning of general academic and domain-specific words or phrases in a text relevant to a *grade 4 topic or subject area*.

RI.4.5 Describe the overall structure (e.g., chronology, comparison, cause/effect, problem/solution) of events, ideas, concepts, or information in a text or part of a text.

RI.4.6 Compare and contrast a firsthand and secondhand account of the same event or topic; describe the differences in focus and the information provided.

RI.4.7 Interpret information presented visually, orally, or quantitatively (e.g., in charts, graphs, diagrams, time lines, animations, or interactive elements on Web pages) and explain how the information contributes to an understanding of the text in which it appears.

RI.4.8 Explain how an author uses reasons and evidence to support particular points in a text.

RI.4.9 Integrate information from two texts on the same topic in order to write or speak about the subject knowledgeably.

RI.4.10 By the end of year, read and comprehend informational texts, including history/social studies, science, and technical texts, in the grades 4–5 text complexity band proficiently, with scaffolding as needed at the high end of the range.

Standards Crosswalk

Third Grade
Reading: Informational Text
Key Ideas and Details
- Refer to text to ask and answer questions to demonstrate understanding.
- Determine the main idea of a text.
- Recount key details and explain how they support the main idea.
- Use appropriate language (time, sequence, cause and effect) to describe the relationship between a series of historical events, scientific ideas or concepts, or steps in technical procedures in a text.

Craft and Structure
- Determine the meaning of general academic and domain-specific words and phrases.
- Use text features and search tools (key words, sidebars, hyperlinks) to locate information.
- Distinguish their own points of view from that of the author of a text.

Integration of Knowledge and Ideas
- Use information gained from illustrations and the words in a text to demonstrate understanding.
- Describe the logical connection between sentences and paragraphs in a text.
- Compare and contrast important points and key details from two texts on the same topic.

Range of Reading and Level of Text Complexity
- By the end of the year, read and comprehend informational texts independently at the high end of the grades 2–3 text complexity band independently and proficiently.

Fifth Grade
Reading: Informational Text
Key Ideas and Details
- Quote direct evidence from a text to explain and draw inferences.
- Determine two or more main ideas and details of a text.
- Summarize the text.
- Explain how people, events, ideas, or concepts are connected in a historical, scientific, or technical text.

Craft and Structure
- Determine the meaning of general academic and domain-specific words and phrases in a text relevant to a grade 5 topic or subject area.
- Compare and contrast the organizational structures in two or more texts.
- Analyze, compare, and contrast different accounts of the same event or topic.

Integration of Knowledge and Ideas
- Efficiently find evidence to support thinking when answering a question or solving a problem.
- Explain how an author uses specific evidence to support each point.
- Use information from different texts to write or speak about subjects knowledgably.

Range of Reading and Level of Text Complexity
- By the end of the year, independently read and comprehend informational texts at the high end of the grades 4–5 text complexity band.

RI.4.1																				
RI.4.2																				
RI.4.3																				
RI.4.4																				
RI.4.5																				
RI.4.6																				
RI.4.7																				
RI.4.8																				
RI.4.9																				
RI.4.10																				

RI.4.1					
RI.4.2					
RI.4.3					
RI.4.4					
RI.4.5					
RI.4.6					
RI.4.7					
RI.4.8					
RI.4.9					
RI.4.10					

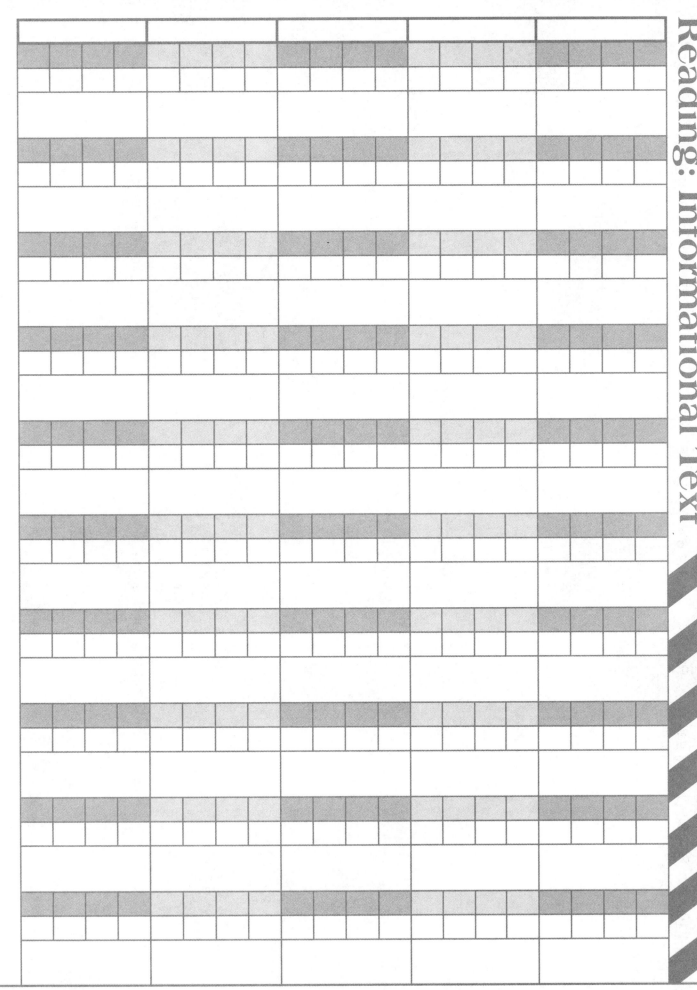

RI.4.1																				
RI.4.2																				
RI.4.3																				
RI.4.4																				
RI.4.5																				
RI.4.6																				
RI.4.7																				
RI.4.8																				
RI.4.9																				
RI.4.10																				

Reading Standards: Foundational Skills

RF.4.1 (Ends in grade 1)

RF.4.2 (Ends in grade 1)

RF.4.3 Know and apply grade-level phonics and word analysis skills in decoding words.
RF.4.3a Use combined knowledge of all letter-sound correspondences, syllabication patterns, and morphology (e.g., roots and affixes) to read accurately unfamiliar multisyllabic words in context and out of context.

RF.4.4 Read with sufficient accuracy and fluency to support comprehension.
RF.4.4a Read grade-level text with purpose and understanding.
RF.4.4b Read grade-level prose and poetry orally with accuracy, appropriate rate, and expression on successive readings.
RF.4.4c Use context to confirm or self-correct word recognition and understanding, rereading as necessary.

Standards Crosswalk

Third Grade
Reading: Foundational Skills
Phonics and Word Recognition
- Decode words using grade-level phonics and word analysis skills.
- Identify and know the meaning of most common prefixes and suffixes.
- Decode words with common Latin suffixes.
- Decode multisyllabic words.
- Read grade-appropriate irregularly spelled words.

Fluency
- Read with sufficient accuracy and fluency to support comprehension.
- Read grade-level text with purpose and understanding.
- Read grade-level prose and poetry with accuracy, appropriate rate, and expression on successive readings.
- Use context and rereading to confirm or self-correct word recognition and understanding.

Fifth Grade
Reading: Foundational Skills
Phonics and Word Recognition
- Know and apply grade-level phonics and word analysis skills to decode words.
- Use all letter-sound correspondences, syllabication patterns, and morphology to read accurately unfamiliar multisyllabic words in context and out of context.

Fluency
- Read with sufficient accuracy and fluency to support comprehension.
- Read grade-level text with purpose and understanding.
- Read grade-level prose and poetry orally with accuracy, appropriate rate, and expression on successive readings.
- Use context and rereading to confirm or self-correct word recognition and understanding.

RF.4.3

RF.4.4

RF.4.3

RF.4.4

RF.4.3

RF.4.4

Writing

W.4.1 Write opinion pieces on topics or texts, supporting a point of view with reasons and information.

    W.4.1a Introduce a topic or text clearly, state an opinion, and create an organizational structure in which related ideas are grouped to support the writer's purpose.

    W.4.1b Provide reasons that are supported by facts and details.

    W.4.1c Link opinion and reasons using words and phrases (e.g., *for instance, in order to, in addition*).

    W.4.1d Provide a concluding statement or section related to the opinion presented.

W.4.2 Write informative/explanatory texts to examine a topic and convey ideas and information clearly.

    W.4.2a Introduce a topic clearly and group related information in paragraphs and sections; include formatting (e.g., headings), illustrations, and multimedia when useful to aiding comprehension.

    W.4.2b Develop the topic with facts, definitions, concrete details, quotations, or other information and examples related to the topic.

    W.4.2c Link ideas within categories of information using words and phrases (e.g., *another, for example, also, because*).

    W.4.2d Use precise language and domain-specific vocabulary to inform about or explain the topic.

    W.4.2e Provide a concluding statement or section related to the information or explanation presented.

W.4.3 Write narratives to develop real or imagined experiences or events using effective technique, descriptive details, and clear event sequences.

    W.4.3a Orient the reader by establishing a situation and introducing a narrator and/or characters; organize an event sequence that unfolds naturally.

    W.4.3b Use dialogue and description to develop experiences and events or show the responses of characters to situations.

    W.4.3c Use a variety of transitional words and phrases to manage the sequence of events.

    W.4.3d Use concrete words and phrases and sensory details to convey experiences and events precisely.

    W.4.3e Provide a conclusion that follows from the narrated experiences or events.

W.4.4 Produce clear and coherent writing in which the development and organization are appropriate to task, purpose, and audience.

W.4.5 With guidance and support from peers and adults, develop and strengthen writing as needed by planning, revising, and editing.

W.4.6 With some guidance and support from adults, use technology, including the Internet, to produce and publish writing as well as to interact and collaborate with others; demonstrate sufficient command of keyboarding skills to type a minimum of one page in a single sitting.

W.4.7 Conduct short research projects that build knowledge through investigation of different aspects of a topic.

W.4.8 Recall relevant information from experiences or gather relevant information from print and digital sources; take notes and categorize information, and provide a list of sources.

W.4.9 Draw evidence from literary or informational texts to support analysis, reflection, and research.

    W.4.9a Apply grade 4 Reading standards to literature (e.g., "Describe in depth a character, setting, or event in a story or drama, drawing on specific details in the text [e.g., a character's thoughts, words, or actions].").

    W.4.9b Apply grade 4 Reading standards to informational texts (e.g., "Explain how an author uses reasons and evidence to support particular points in a text").

W.4.10 Write routinely over extended time frames (time for research, reflection, and revision) and shorter time frames (a single sitting or a day or two) for a range of discipline-specific tasks, purposes, and audiences.

Standards Crosswalk

Third Grade
Writing
Text Types and Purposes
- Write opinion pieces, supporting a point of view with reasons.
- Introduce the topic or text, states an opinion, and lists reasons in an organized manner; provide reasons to support the opinion; use linking words and phrases to connect opinion and reasons; provide a concluding statement or section.
- Write informative/explanatory texts to examine a topic and convey ideas and information clearly.
- Introduce a topic, group related information, and include illustrations when useful; develop the topic with facts, definitions, and details; use linking words and phrases to connect ideas; provide a concluding statement or section.
- Write real or imaginary narratives using effective technique, details, and clear sequences.
- Establish a situation and introduce a narrator and/or characters; organize a natural even sequence; uses dialogue, and describe the actions, thoughts and feelings of characters in response to situations; use temporal words and phrases to signal event order; provide closure.

Production and Distribution of Writing
With guidance and support:
- Develop, organize, and produce writing appropriate to task and purpose.
- Develop and strengthen writing by planning, revising, and editing.
- Use technology to produce and publish writing (using keyboarding skills), including in collaboration.

Research to Build and Present Knowledge
- Conduct research to build knowledge about a topic.
- Recall information from experiences or gather information from print and digital sources.
- Take brief notes on sources and sort evidence into provided categories.

Range of Writing
- Routinely write for a range of discipline-specific tasks, purposes, and audiences.

Fifth Grade
Writing
Text Types and Purposes
- Write opinion pieces, supporting a point of view with reasons and information.
- Introduce the topic or text clearly, state an opinion, and use an organized structure that groups related ideas; provide logically-ordered reasons supported by facts and details; use linking words, phrases, and clauses to connect opinion and reasons; provide a related conclusion.
- Write informative/explanatory texts to examine a topic and convey ideas and information clearly.
- Introduce a topic clearly; provide a general observation and focus, group related information in paragraphs and sections and include formatting, illustrations, and multimedia when useful; develop the topic with facts, definitions, concrete details, quotations, and other relevant information; use linking words, phrases, and clauses to connect ideas; provide a related conclusion.
- Write real or imaginary narratives using effective technique, details, and clear sequences.
- Establish a situation and introduce a narrator and/or characters; organize a natural event sequence; uses dialogue, description, and pacing to develop experiences, events, and characters' responses to situations; use transitional words, phrases, and clauses to manage the sequence of events; use concrete words, phrases, and sensory details to convey experiences and events precisely; provide a conclusion that follows from the events.

Production and Distribution of Writing
- Produce coherent writing with development and organization appropriate to task and purpose.
- With guidance and support, develop and strengthen writing by planning, revising, editing, or rewriting.
- With some guidance and support, use technology to produce and publish writing and to interact and collaborate; demonstrate sufficient keyboarding skills to type at least two pages in a sitting.

Research to Build and Present Knowledge
- Conduct short research projects using several sources that build knowledge about a topic.
- Recall relevant information from experiences or gather information from print and digital sources.
- Summarize or paraphrase information in notes and writing, and provide a list of sources.
- Draw evidence from texts to support analysis, reflection, and research.

Range of Writing
- Routinely write for a range of discipline-specific tasks, purposes, and audiences.

W.4.1																				
W.4.2																				
W.4.3																				
W.4.4																				
W.4.5																				
W.4.6																				
W.4.7																				
W.4.8																				
W.4.9																				
W.4.10																				

72

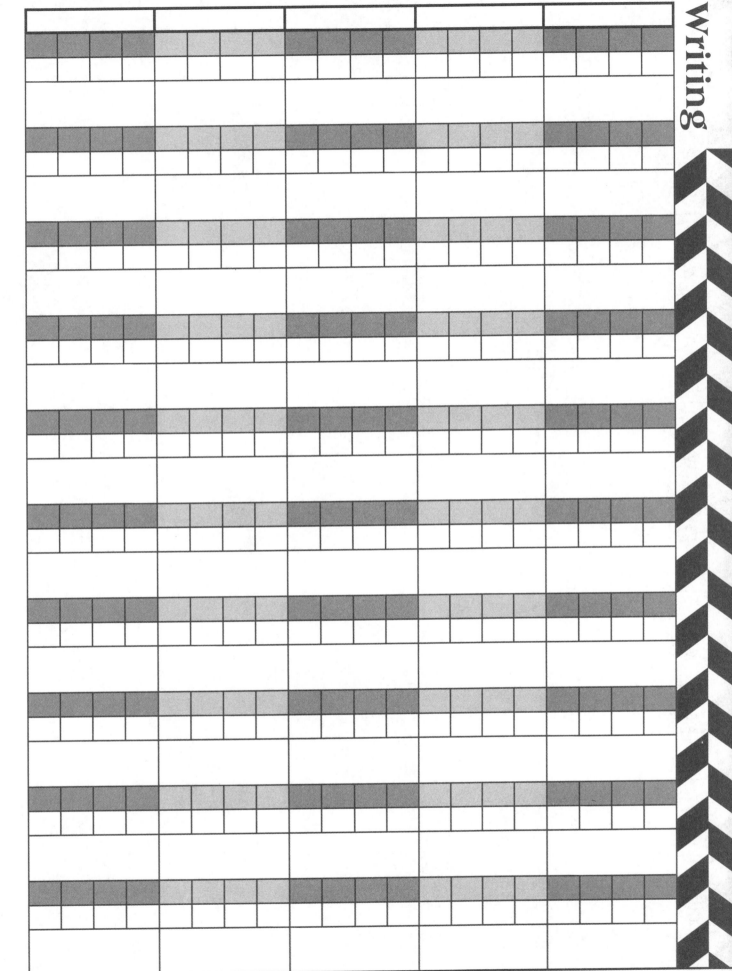

W.4.1					
W.4.2					
W.4.3					
W.4.4					
W.4.5					
W.4.6					
W.4.7					
W.4.8					
W.4.9					
W.4.10					

W.4.1					
W.4.2					
W.4.3					
W.4.4					
W.4.5					
W.4.6					
W.4.7					
W.4.8					
W.4.9					
W.4.10					

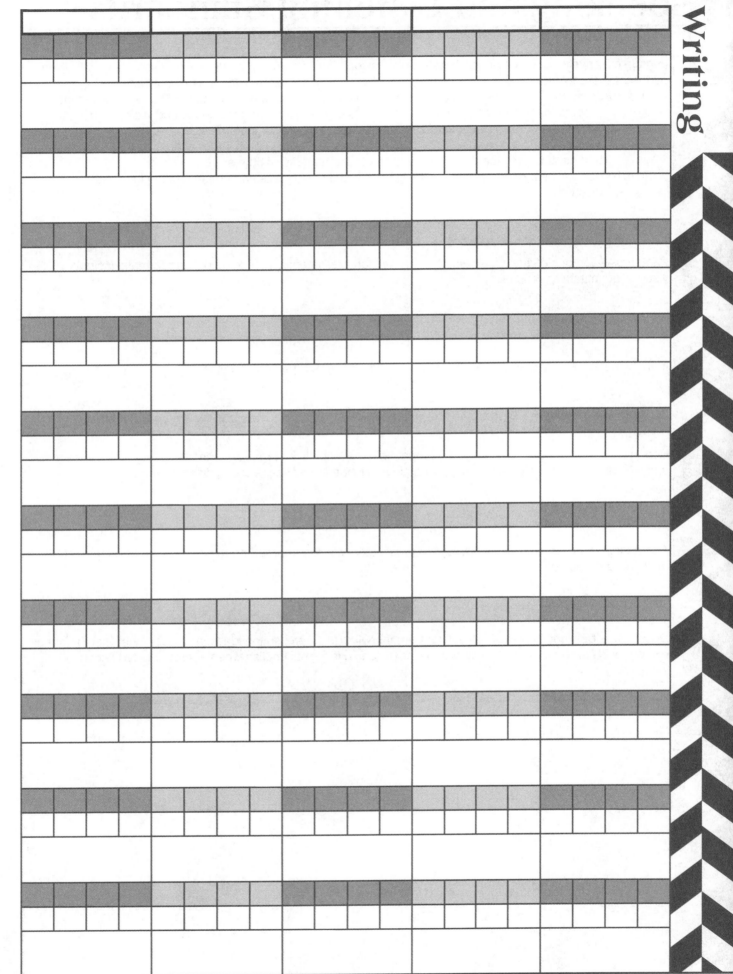

Speaking and Listening Standards

SL.4.1
Engage effectively in a range of collaborative discussions (one-on-one, in groups, and teacher-led) with diverse partners on *grade 4 topics and texts*, building on others' ideas and expressing their own clearly.
- SL.4.1a Come to discussions prepared, having read or studied required material; explicitly draw on that preparation and other information known about the topic to explore ideas under discussion.
- SL.4.1b Follow agreed-upon rules for discussions and carry out assigned roles.
- SL.4.1c Pose and respond to specific questions to clarify or follow up on information, and make comments that contribute to the discussion and link to the remarks of others.
- SL.4.1d Review the key ideas expressed and explain their own ideas and understanding in light of the discussion.

SL.4.2
Paraphrase portions of a text read aloud or information presented in diverse media and formats, including visually, quantitatively, and orally.

SL.4.3
Identify the reasons and evidence a speaker provides to support particular points.

SL.4.4
Report on a topic or text, tell a story, or recount an experience in an organized manner, using appropriate facts and relevant, descriptive details to support main ideas or themes; speak clearly at an understandable pace.

SL.4.5
Add audio recordings and visual displays to presentations when appropriate to enhance the development of main ideas or themes.

SL.4.6
Differentiate between contexts that call for formal English (e.g., presenting ideas) and situations where informal discourse is appropriate (e.g., small-group discussion); use formal English when appropriate to task and situation.

Standards Crosswalk

Third Grade

Speaking and Listening

Comprehension and Collaboration

- Participate in collaborative discussions on grade 3 topics and texts.
- Prepare for discussions and participate appropriately.
- Follow agreed-upon rules for discussions.
- Ask questions to clarify information presented, stay on topic, and offer relevant comments.
- Explain their own ideas and understanding in light of a discussion.
- Determine the main ideas and supporting details of a text read aloud or multimedia presentations.
- Ask and answer questions about information from a speaker, offering appropriate elaboration.

Presentation of Knowledge and Ideas

- Speak clearly at an understandable pace to report on a topic or text, tell a story, or recount an experience with appropriate facts and descriptive details.
- Create audio recordings of stories or poems that demonstrate fluency and appropriate pacing.
- Add visual displays when needed to enhance certain facts or details.
- Speak in complete sentences when appropriate to provide requested detail or clarification.

Fifth Grade

Speaking and Listening

Comprehension and Collaboration

- Participate in collaborative discussions on grade 5 topics and texts, building on others' ideas and expressing their own clearly.
- Come prepared to discussions, having read or studied material, drawing on that preparation to explore ideas under discussion.
- Follow agreed-upon rules for discussions and carry out assigned roles.
- Ask and answer questions and make comments that contribute to the discussion.
- Review the key ideas expressed and draw conclusions in light of the discussion.
- Summarize a written text read aloud or information presented in diverse media and formats.
- Summarize and explain the reasons and evidence supporting points a speaker makes.

Presentation of Knowledge and Ideas

- Report on a topic or text or present an opinion, sequencing ideas logically and using appropriate facts and relevant, descriptive details.
- Speak clearly at an understandable pace.
- Include multimedia components and visual displays in presentations when appropriate.
- Adapt speech to a variety of contexts and tasks, using formal English when appropriate.

SL.4.1					
SL.4.2					
SL.4.3					
SL.4.4					
SL.4.5					
SL.4.6					

SL.4.1				
SL.4.2				
SL.4.3				
SL.4.4				
SL.4.5				
SL.4.6				

SL.4.1					
SL.4.2					
SL.4.3					
SL.4.4					
SL.4.5					
SL.4.6					

84

Language Standards

L.4.1

Demonstrate command of the conventions of standard English grammar and usage when writing or speaking.

- L.4.1a Use relative pronouns (*who, whose, whom, which, that*) and relative adverbs (*where, when, why*).
- L.4.1b Form and use the progressive (e.g., *I was walking*; *I am walking*; *I will be walking*) verb tenses.
- L.4.1c Use modal auxiliaries (e.g., *can, may, must*) to convey various conditions.
- L.4.1d Order adjectives within sentences according to conventional patterns (e.g., *a small red bag* rather than *a red small bag*).
- L.4.1e Form and use prepositional phrases.
- L.4.1f Produce complete sentences, recognizing and correcting inappropriate fragments and run-ons.
- L.4.1g Correctly use frequently confused words (e.g., *to, too, two*; *there, their*).

L.4.2

Demonstrate command of the conventions of standard English capitalization, punctuation, and spelling when writing.

- L.4.2a Use correct capitalization.
- L.4.2b Use commas and quotation marks to mark direct speech and quotations from a text.
- L.4.2c Use a comma before a coordinating conjunction in a compound sentence.
- L.4.2d Spell grade-appropriate words correctly, consulting references as needed.

L.4.3

Use knowledge of language and its conventions when writing, speaking, reading, or listening.

- L.4.3a Choose words and phrases to convey ideas precisely.
- L.4.3b Choose punctuation for effect.
- L.4.3c Differentiate between contexts that call for formal English (e.g., presenting ideas) and situations where informal discourse is appropriate (e.g., small-group discussion).

L.4.4

Determine or clarify the meaning of unknown and multiple-meaning word and phrases based on grade 4 reading and content, choosing flexibly from a range of strategies.

- L.4.4a Use context (e.g., definitions, examples, or restatements in text) as a clue to the meaning of a word or phrase.
- L.4.4b Use common, grade-appropriate Greek and Latin affixes and roots as clues to the meaning of a word (e.g., *telegraph, photograph, autograph*).
- L.4.4c Consult reference materials (e.g., dictionaries, glossaries, thesauruses), both print and digital, to find the pronunciation and determine or clarify the precise meaning of key words and phrases.

L.4.5

Demonstrate understanding of figurative language, word relationships, and nuances in word meanings.

- L.4.5a Explain the meaning of simple similes and metaphors (e.g., *as pretty as a picture*) in context.
- L.4.5b Recognize and explain the meaning of common idioms, adages, and proverbs.
- L.4.5c Demonstrate understanding of words by relating them to their opposites (antonyms) and to words with similar but not identical meanings (synonyms).

L.4.6

Acquire and use accurately grade-appropriate general academic and domain-specific words and phrases, including those that signal precise actions, emotions, or states of being (e.g., *quizzed, whined, stammered*) and that are basic to a particular topic (e.g., *wildlife, conservation*, and *endangered* when discussing animal preservation).

Standards Crosswalk

Third Grade
Language
Conventions of Standard English
- Use conventions of standard English grammar and usage in writing or speaking.
- Understand and explain the function of nouns, pronouns, verbs, adjectives, and adverbs; form and use regular and irregular plural nouns; use abstract nouns; form and use regular and irregular verbs, and simple verb tenses; ensure subject-verb and pronoun-antecedent agreement; form and use comparative and superlative adjectives and adverbs correctly; use coordinating and subordinating conjunctions.
- Produce simple, compound, and complex sentences.
- Use capitalization, punctuation, and spelling correctly when writing.
- Capitalize appropriate words in titles; use commas in addresses; use commas and quotation marks in dialogue; form and use possessives.
- Use conventional spelling and spelling patterns to write words and to add suffixes to base words; consult reference materials to check and correct spellings.

Knowledge of Language
- Choose words and phrases for effect.
- Recognize differences between spoken and written standard English.

Vocabulary Acquisition and Use
- Flexibly use various strategies to understand unknown words on a third-grade level.
- Use sentence-level context as a clue to the meaning of a word or phrase; find the meaning of a new word when a known affix is added to a known word; use known root words to determine the meaning of an unknown word with same root; use glossaries or beginning dictionaries to clarify meaning.
- Understand figurative language, word relationships, and nuances in words.
- Distinguish the literal and nonliteral meanings of words and phrases in context.
- Identify real-life connections between words and their uses.
- Distinguish meaning among words that describe states of mind or certainty.
- Learn and use conversational, academic, and subject-specific vocabulary, including words that show time and place.

Fifth Grade
Language
Conventions of Standard English
- Use conventions of standard English grammar and usage in writing or speaking.
- Explain the function of conjunctions, prepositions, and interjections; form and use the perfect verb tenses; use verb tense to convey various times, sequences, states, and conditions; recognize and correct inappropriate shifts in verb tense; use correlative conjunctions.
- Use capitalization, punctuation, and spelling correctly when writing.
- Use punctuation to separate items in a series; use a comma to separate an introductory element from the rest of the sentence; use a comma to set off introductory words or phrases and questions, and to indicate direct address; use underlining, quotation marks, or italics to indicate titles of works.
- Spell grade-appropriate words correctly, consulting references as needed.

Knowledge of Language
- Use knowledge of language when writing, speaking, reading, or listening.
- Expand, combine, and reduce sentences for meaning, audience interest, and style.
- Compare and contrast the varieties of English used in stories, dramas, or poems.

Vocabulary Acquisition and Use
- Use various strategies to determine the meaning of unfamiliar words or phrases.
- Use context as a clue to the meaning of a word or phrase; use common Greek and Latin affixes and roots as clues to the meanings of words; consult reference materials to find the pronunciation and meaning of key words.
- Understand figurative language, word relationships, and nuances in word meaning in context; recognize the meaning of idioms, adages, and proverbs.
- Use the relationships between words to better understand each word.
- Learn and use academic and subject-specific vocabulary, including words that signal contrast, addition, and other logical relationships.

L.4.1

L.4.2

L.4.3

L.4.4

L.4.5

L.4.6

L.4.1

L.4.2

L.4.3

L.4.4

L.4.5

L.4.6

© Carson-Dellosa CD-104803

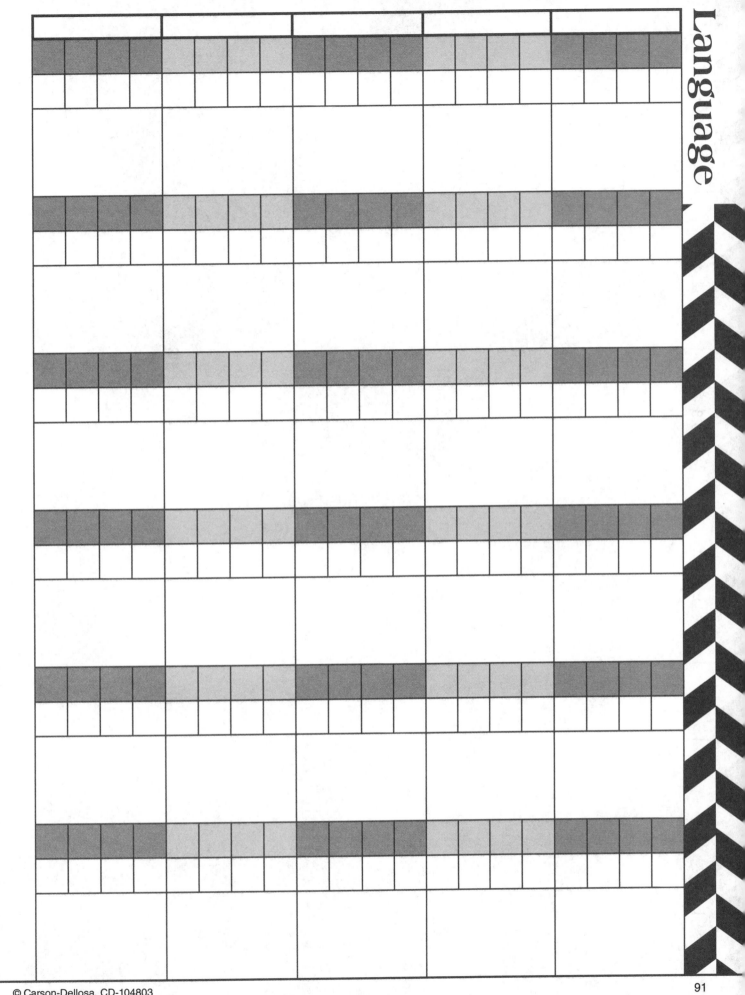

L.4.1

L.4.2

L.4.3

L.4.4

L.4.5

L.4.6

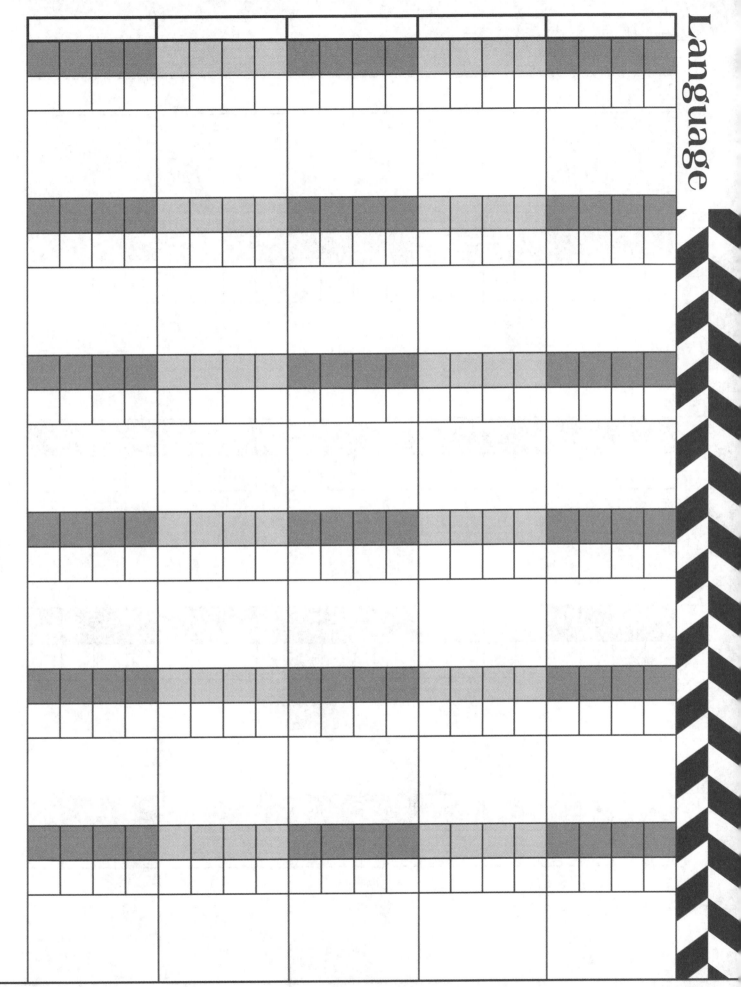

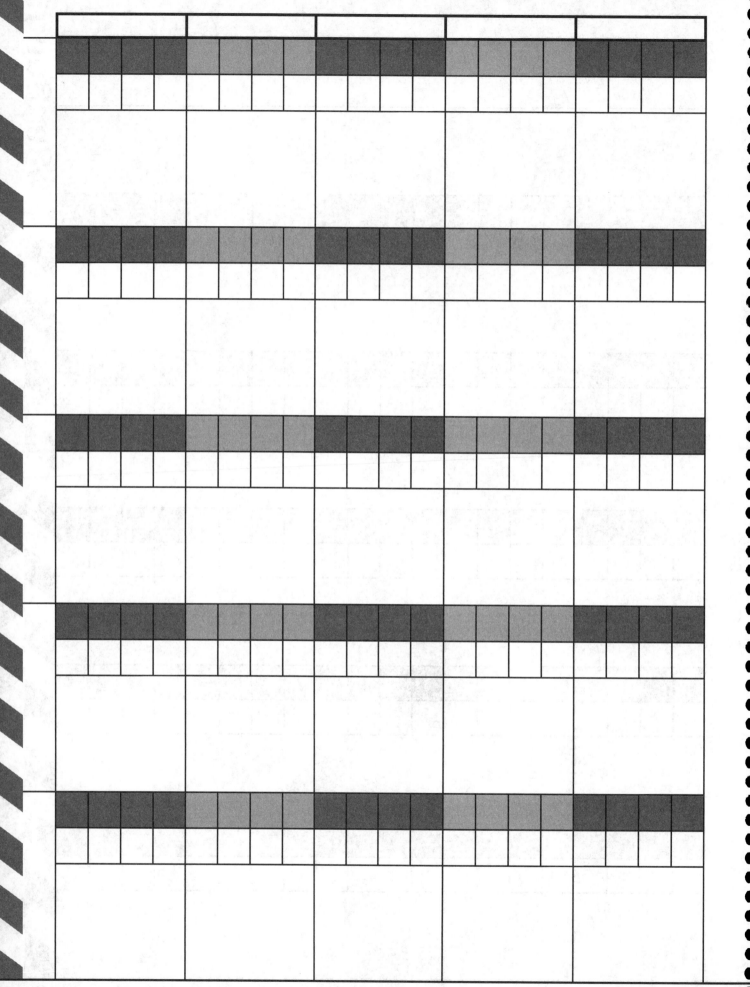

94

Name _____ **Date** _____

Standard _____

Notes